The Wonders Of The Cozmos

By Casey LaRios

Published by The Wizitch Company

Whatyamaycallit?

Call it whatever you
wish, we are all kids
of the same life-force.
The Sol's of Spirit*
The Alien-Elders that
planted us here? They
use to laugh at me,
now they laugh with

me, or cry because
they lost me. O well.
It's all right, except for
what's wrong. You are
always on the right
path & always will be-
As long as you listen
to your guts'
instincts & live your
dreams in the greatest

high the best you can.
Stick your tung out,
get sum Spirit-
Powers. Trix +

Unjulation : The art
of moving fluidly. Go
with the flo. Like the
SEE. Everything is
perfect. It's nice to
know it. Thanx for the

tips. Loud & Quiet. Not too fast, not too slow, but betwixt, in the middle. The Center. This is where I live. Always+ Cattitude is everything. As well as being in rightness. Righteousness. The crown. You may find me at The Thirsty Crow down by Silver Lake, sipn' on holy spirits with The Curry Cowboy. Or at The Wizdom Tree with Mr Gumball, the highest hill in The Holy Woods, where the psykic Powers are. Or rocking the sands on the beaches of Angel City. And that's just what's local. There are non-local spaces I journey to, as well. I live to journey. Wouldn't have it any other way. The

Rolling Stones we're wrong about something. You CAN always get what you want. Maybe not right when you want it, but you will, if you really truly wish. In this life or another. It's not on our time,

there is no time really.
All is cozmic order,
the energy-space of
The Cozmos. Yes * so
happy we met.

On & Up

You & you alone know
what's best for you.

No one else loves me as good as I do. I'm you. Like the cat says, MeYou. Nobody out there is above you in intelligence or any other way. I got sea sick on a water bed. Meeting the wizard of Oz in the

woods & flying to
SEE. All systems go.
Green light. First in,
first out. Talking
secret in other-worldly
tungz. O , well. Down
at the Well. Love what
you've done with the
place. Today we
created a movie

concept for a new TV show. I have to say, it was the best gig of my life, so far... SEE. Circus Space Camp. SuperNatural. The dream job. I found what people come to Hollywood to find. What a trip. Thanks for the ryde, Asid. See you on the next one, friends. Spirit says, 'this & greater thing will you do!' Dam, what's better than STAR-TREK? I'm excited! Seeing without eyes. Keep your eyes on the balls... Have fun. That's the most important thing. Thanx RingMasters, for whipping me into ship-shape. And thanx Earth-Land, for all your wild love + support. Welcome to Heaven *

The Celebration Of
The Circle =

It's a bittersweet trip
this time around. The
family gathers in a
gathering to honor the
life & death? - of Papa,
The Wizard Of The

Woods. The Family Tree will never be the same. The day he passed was mystical. There was a meteor shower the night he left us, & on my birthday. He told me he wanted to take off on a comet. I'm now the new Wizitch. It's a big responsibility, it's the best responsibility. So sick of these but's. Yes, but... It's great, but... I do, but... Don't you use your butt enough? You don't have to talk about it all day. Shut up more often. O well... It's your life. I love everything, & it's funny. Camping in the woods tonight, or at least that's the plan. Things change. I'm jazzed! Cats don't use sleeping bagz, do they? Green curry, mushroom juice, & rainbows. Charging up @ Yee Old Oaks so we have enough juice, & Hindu Kush through the night. This is my 1st time spending the night out here. Its going to be a majikal eve!

Promise * On-to new
sees...

The Cat-Dragon's Lair
+

It's really nice being
woken up by the
sounds of who'ing
owls, dancing

lizards, singing ravens, playing critters, the holy river, & the sweet breezy whispering in the trees. Zen. As if you could describe it with words, you can't really. Peace. Wayyyy up in The Cat-

Dragon's Lair. In The castle, where the majik is kooked up. Yes. What works for me probably won't work for you. What works for her probably won't work for him. So on... We are all 1 being, & we are also individual 'i's. Weird right? One cozmic consciousness, many expressions of it. One sun = zillions of different rA's of light. The same 1 electricity running a variety of unique instruments. I think of the cozmos

as a big mind. This
universe & all the
other ones. A Master
Mind. I believe that's
what it is. Thoughts
make things.
Feelings do dealings.
Karma is action.
Great actions create
great reactions.

Would you treat
yourself like that? Be
the 1%. The Keeper Of
The Circle.

The Sage & The
Talking Back-Pack.

One day, my back-
pack started talking
to me. It said,

"Hey Jackass! Wake
the fuck up! Quit
wacking off & go pick
the sacred sage in
The Holy Woods. The
Tribes Of The Villages

of The Worlds Of The Sols need it, to bring peace..."

'I don't know where it is.'

"Find it! You are wizer than you know,

& you have super-
powers!"

'Ok.'

So I went. I seeked
high, low, &
medium...
Everywhere! What felt
like eons had passed

me by. The treasure I spent my life looking for was always just right out of reach, escaping me. I felt it was close now. So close I could smell it. I could SEE it in my minds eye. Finally, I found it! Lots of it...

From: nothing To: everything. I picked it up & shared it with The Tribes Of The Villages Of The Worlds Of The Sols. Then, my talking back-pack said, ...

"Yes! You did it. You made The Tribes Of The Villages Of The Worlds Of The Sols really happy. The cozmos smiles on you. Now, there is nothing more to do. Just, BE."

'Thanx, bag...'

"Welcome..."

My back-pack never talked to me again. I guess it didn't have anything else to say.

The beginning...

The Search Party Is Over

It's a good thing, too, because we're really fucking tired of this shit. The treasure that we've been seeking for eons & has always eluded us, has been found. We outsmarted the dumb goblins. Paradise. Glad that's over... Lets never lose the gold again, OK? Digging it all back up is a big pain in the ass. AAA, now I can relax. Thankyou spirit, for all the love. Iloveyou * A big Cat-Man told me 1 penny is worth 1 million dollars, it's all 1. I was paid 11 cents today so I really made $ 11,000,000.00. Sold the art, alas! It feels really, really, really

great. It's nice to have
so much money I do
know what to do with.
Money = Freedom.
Now I can really help -
share better than ever,
give more food & water
& homes to the poor,
help the family. Yes!

Rainbows for
everyone... So it is ~

In A World Of Yes &
No

Life is kind & krewl.
Beautiful & ugly.
High & low. Hot &
cold. Light & Dark.

Can't have one
without the other... or
can you? Maybe the
flowers bloom best in
peace. Just maybe,
there is no need to
struggle, or reason to
suffer. Did you know
that working hard is
a myth made by

monkeys? As old as the hills... How old are the hills, the terra of Earth, anyway? Something tells me not as old as we've been told. The worlds, more & more, seem to be built architectures. Made-up Mansions.

Things aren't what they seem. I agree. Hardly anything is as it seems, but is as it is. It is what it is & it isn't what it isn't. Interesting. How do we know what's really real? Set the Sol a-blaze, schmelt, what

remains is real. Be as true to you as positively possible, be perfect, & what meets you there is the Truth I bet, but don't gamble. Power comes to you. Be the best *
All I hear is the bells of angels & the sweet

muzik of Spirit. Dear Spirit, tell me what I need to know, show me what I need to see. Thanx, for all the love. Iloveyou + Keep ryding. We made it. Next stop, Family Tavern. Rock-A-Lot.

Yes, mam. I will. IAM.
How are you?
Do you believe in
shape-shifters? Beings
that can shift their
shape, even change
colors? I do. I've seen
some super strange
phenomena, so why
not? Balls of bright,

awesome light,
spaceships, flying in
the sky &
disappearing at will.
Ethers of energy that
stur around in my
room, in the quantum
air. Majikal creatures
coming into my
dream-life with

powerful messages
from the beyond.
Insights of Sages
traveling 1,000 miles
/ 1 second, in a
Starlight super steed.
Things that defy
logic & reason, & this
is just the beginning!
Majik is everywhere,

in the cozmos. You are a creator, the creator, of your life. You are the commander of the cozmos, The Controller. It's all you - All of it. 1 ~ The Gold Law : treat 'others' as you'd want them to treat you.

That's it. Why, then, the badness? I would never act like that. Life shows you ALL it's personality potentials, you choose which way to go. Death's a choice, as is Life. To be, or not to be... Tragedy is only neglect & bad parenting. There are no problems, only solutions. The question is the answer. Everything is perfect. Stay righteous. Sin isn't allowed in Spirits tipi. Just, peace. So it is.

Funny, all sin really means is to miss the mark. Like an arrow (thought) missing the target. Go again. Go until you get it right. Bulls-eye! So happy we got over the ditch. You experience what you focus on. What do you SEE? In the sky, anywhere, you can SEE anything if you look close enough. Yes + SEE you soon.

The Aggravation's Of Pollution & The Gold Standards Of

Ridiculous
Expectations •

Gently fierce, like
fire, water, earth, air,
ether... All the
elements. You get
what you give. Ryde
& fly, or not. It's all
up to you. Va, Ra, Ca.

I don't know what
that means. It's
probably a crow song.
I saw a white dragon
in the sky, at first I
thought it was a
cloud. I'd love to take
it out for a ryde! Also
want a pet Raven.
KAA! It'll be so good

ass. Excited! The little trickster. She'll come with me everywhere I go & tell me jokes, scare the demons off. The key is to have the egg right as it hatches so you are the 1st thing it sees. The Raven will SEE you

as the Lord. Mommy
+ Daddy. A weird
space sound came
from out of nowhere,
just above my head.
Strange muzik of the
cozmos. Singing
from out of the blue.
Super cool. Muzik
teaches me how to live.

Muzik is prayer. Relience. Religion + Science says the essence of the cozmos is sound. I'd have to agree & obey. Also, know when to disobey. As Truman says in the movie ARMAGEDDON,

"This is one order you shouldn't follow & you fucking know it!"

The Tipi ~ In The Jungle

Trekking into the jungle tonight to sleep

at the Tipi. At least,
that's the plan.
Things change. I feel
like a freakin' Girl
Scout. Want a cookie?
They're vegan.
Animals are people
not products. I stopped
eating my family a
long time ago. I was

raised wrong, but now I know what's right. Whatever works - it works if you work it. The cool thing about being in your own space is not having any dumb-ass rules to deal with. It's the best! Freedom....

Happy Sun Day. It's the best day ever. My cousins wife didn't appreciate my sunburned face skin flakes on the bathroom floor of their apartment where I was staying in Hollywood. She got upset that I didn't pick up after myself & clean up my mess. I didn't even know it happened. Sorry my decomposing bothers you. Not sorry. Bye! It's amazing, no matter what, people will always find

something wrong
with you. It comes
from their own
insecurity. Energy
doesn't lie. People
aren't always people,
tho. They may look
like people, but be an
even lower, or way
higher, entity. There

are mixed levels In these earth school classes... Be aware. You know better. Thirst-Quenched. What does a dinosaur say? RAW! I wonder how natural nature really is. I feel it's 1/3 natural, 1/3 un-

natural, 1/3 super-
natural. 3. The Holy
Trinity. Makes sense
to me... Today I'll go
pick a bag of sage for
the family, the
village. I love my jobz.
So thankful I get to
do the dream work.
Not everyone gets the

chance, so I'm honored. Blest. Yes. Zen. So many wish they had your life. Be thankful... A conspiracy of crows follows me down the trail, guiding the way. Like an entourage of angels.

Beautiful beauty.
Wow* Rainbows
everywhere! Good
thing I have cat eyes. I
SEE better in the
dark. It's adorable how
Venus cozy's up with
mama. The sweetest
thing, family. Mana.
So lost without the

jam. The Tribe.
Thanx, dear spirit, for
all the love. I feel like
a majik Cat-Dragon.
Guess I am. The
muzik keeps coming
in sweeter & sweeter &
sweeter. Now what?
Whatever I want.
That's the kool thing.

The journey in the
unknown, my happy
space. Bats... I will.
Take care, no one will
just give it to you,
well, sometimes. Ask,
its given. You get
what you give. The
Law Of The Cozmos
~ What you SEE is

what you get. Simple. The director told me to forget my practice. So what the fuck am I suppose to do, not practice? Play differently than usual. Confusing sense. I get it. Un-learn what you

learned & be a blank,
empty canvas so the
colors of Life can
come in & play. Forget
to Re-member. A
Paradox. Ring Of The
Lords. Keeper Of The
Circle. Only peace
comes into our life.
Yes. The opposite of a

weapon is peaceful in-
action. Zen. Wish I
had kool witches to be
with right now. So it
is. Here they come...
Grew into my Cat-
Dragon tail today.
DreamWork. To the
next level! Instead of
breathing fire, I blow

rainbows. SEE deep, go deep. Not too deep! but deep. The candles are lit. I realized the guitar is a generator of energy. The energy of the art is the source of our wealth. Always. 777 = 21 = 3 ***

It's not about

winning anymore.
Royalty is gone.
We're in the same ship
here. It's about
everyone being a
winner. Happy +
Healthy + Helpy +
The Village, all
working together as
One. Team Work

makes the Dream Work. I don't think you find your real purpose, it finds you. Take care of Life & Life will take care of you. When seeking answers, One has to quiet the sol. Survival of the wittiest.

Something special
happens to you when
you sleep in the trees.
The spirits & elements
of nature energize the
sol with a wonderful
rooting baptism you
can't find hiding
behind walls, bars,
gates & locks. It comes

to you, outside of in-
security, when your
out in the open, in the
clear. High visibility.
Natural. Present.
Treat the present like
a gift, because it is.
Just got the chills. If
you haven't kissed the
world lately, you

really should +
iloveyou

Peace + plenty

Everything is perfect
Every ones wishes in
the highest good
coming true, NOW

We live in The Castle

All is Now

Lots Of Love

So it is...

!